What's a Sampler?

W9-BOK-701

by Freff

Edited by
K. Kimball
Holland

A basic guide to the world of digital sampling

 Hal Leonard Publishing Corporation

7777 West Bluemound Road P.O. Box 13819 Milwaukee, WI 53213

ISBN 0-88188-883-4

Table of Contents

1

What is Sampling?

The answer to the question above is simple: Sampling is magic—only it's the magic of computer chips and lighting-fast digital audio, not genies and bottles. It's a whole new musical technology that makes it possible for you to play literally any sound you can hear—not just a synthesized approximation, but the actual sound itself, from the massed voices of the Mormon Tabernacle Choir to a solo violin to the croaking of a pond full of frogs.

With the right gear, you can play any sound in the world by "sampling" it.

Sampling, you see, is just another word for "recording"—but a special type of recording that offers marvelous musical possibilities to anyone who takes a little time to learn how (and why) it works.

2

Basics of Sound

To fully understand sampling it helps to look closely at something we usually take for granted: sound.

Sound is waves of changing air pressure. That's all. Hit a drum, bow a string, kick a can,...whatever you do to create sound generates vibrations, which in turn create changes in air pressure, which travel in waves from the sound source to your ear.

SOUND: FROM SOURCE TO SENSATION

We can neatly capture these patterns, or *waveforms*, in diagrams like the following:

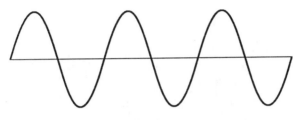

WAVEFORM DIAGRAM

The curving line in this diagram marks changes in air pressure over time. The straight line running from left to right represents zero change—i.e., no sound at all. As you can see, the pressure gets greater than normal as the waveform goes all the way up and lower than normal as it goes all the way down, and it repeats this cycle of alternating pressure quite regularly

You can tell a lot about a sound by looking at its waveform. For example, the height of the wave above that zero line tells you how loud the sound is:

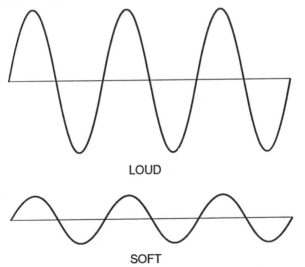

LOUD

SOFT

In the diagrams above, the first sound is clearly much louder than the second.

You can also tell whether a sound is pitched or is just noise:

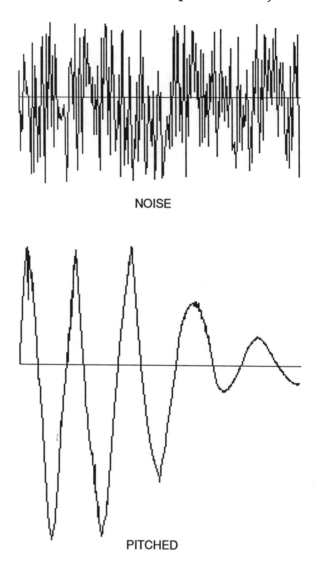

NOISE

PITCHED

Waveforms that are irregular and do not repeat, like the top one above, we hear as noise. But waveforms with repeating patterns, like the bottom one, we hear as pitched sounds. Each repeating portion of a waveform is known as a *cycle*; pitch is indicated by number of times a cycle repeats per second. The faster the cycles go by, the higher the pitch:

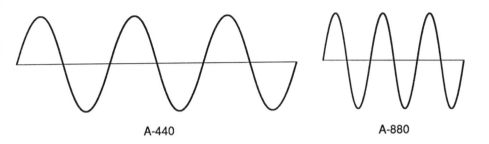

A-440   A-880

In the diagram above you can see the same waveform as it would look at both concert A (440 cycles per second) and exactly one octave up (880 cycles per second). That's one of the Big Rules of Vibration, by the way: our ears hear pitch *exponentially*, not *linearly*. For every octave a waveform rises in pitch, the number of cycles per second doubles.

One last thing to take note of: as well as revealing volume and pitch, waveforms give strong clued about *timbre* (also called *tone color*). Different sounds have different timbres: a flute and a piano, both playing concert A, do not sound alike, and their waveforms show us why:

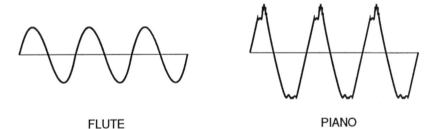

FLUTE   PIANO

The piano has more *overtones* (also called *harmonics*) than the flute, resulting in a more complicated waveform. Overtones are important, and we'll be coming back to them later in this book. For now, a handy rule of thumb to remember is that the more complex the repeating cycle of a waveform, the richer and more interesting the sound.

3

Basics of Digital Recording

Now lets stir some technical wizardry in along with the natural magic of the world. It's time to look at what happens when you digitally "sample" a sound.

The key word here is "digital." As in digital recording, digital synthesizers, digital compact discs...all slightly different, but related, technologies based on the idea that even complicated waveforms can be represented by a simple pattern of 0's and 1's—and without 99% of the problems that bedevil analog recording, such as wow, flutter, rumble, and tape hiss.

Here's how digital recording works: It starts like all recording, with a sound. The audio energy in this sound is measured thousands of times per second by a microprocessor. Each of these measurements is a single sample. They aren't sound; they're just numbers. But taken together they create a mathematical picture of the recorded sound, and if you play all of them back through a DAC (Digital-to-Analog Converter) you'll able able to hear the original source.

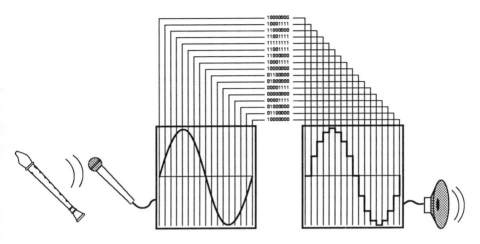

ANALOG TO DIGITAL AND BACK AGAIN

Of course, if there were nothing more to sampling than just recording and playing back, it wouldn't be confusing at all. But it would also be of limited use, as we'll see in the next section.

4

Types of Sampling Instruments

The commonest sample-based musical instruments are *digital drum machines*. Expensive rarities when first released, you can now choose from many high-quality, low priced models. While features may vary from instrument to instrument, they all have one thing in common—ROM (Read-Only Memory) chips containing digital recordings of various drums and percussion. Most also have a significant limitation, which is that you can't use them to record your own samples. In all but higher-priced models, the only way to change sounds is to change chips, and sometimes you can't even do that.

If you have small amounts of RAM (Random-Access Memory) memory in place of ROMs, you can catch your own samples on the fly, for echo, chorusing, and one-shot effects. This kind of device is known as a *sampling digital delay line*. Typically they come in rackmount form. As with drum machines, sampling DDLs started out expensive but have decreased considerably in price.

More powerful than digital drum machines and sampling DDLs are full-blown samplers.

In these instruments, *available memory* is important, because memory is sound. It's that simple. The more RAM an instrument has, the more sound it can store to work with. A little memory, as in a drum machine, is enough for a few drumbeats. But it won't let you recreate the full range of a pennywhistle or a piano. For that you need a lot more—and memory isn't cheap.

The other thing these instruments need is *processing power* (brains, you might say). The smarter an instrument is, the more it can do with its sampled sounds. But smarts don't came cheap either.

The result is something of a juggling act. To make an affordable high-quality instrument means making certain compromises. It means using processing power creatively to get around memory limits, or—conversely—giving up some features and a wide on-board selection of timbres in return for better imitation of a specific sound, such as the piano.

It also means that for *you* to get the most from your sampling instruments, you'll have to learn where these limits lie. If you don't, you won't be able to finagle your way around them.

5

Recording Good Samples

The essence of recording good samples is simple. In fact, it's pretty much the same as making any good recording. You want the cleanest signal you can get, and that signal should be recorded at the highest level possible (short of distortion). If dealing with acoustic sounds, you still use the same microphones and mike techniques. If dealing with synths, you still go direct-inject. If sampling a buzz-saw lead guitar, you still crank up the same amp.

Of course, there are a few differences:

- Your sound source—instrument output, microphone, sound effects record, whatever—is plugged directly into the AUDIO IN jack on your sampler, or patched there via your mixing board.

- You have to pay attention to all the settings in the LCD readout of the sampler, then think about the sound being sampled, and finally make deliberate choices concerning things like *trigger level* and *sampling rate* and *sampling time*.

- You might have to make certain EQ adjustments in light of your sampling choices.

Otherwise, it's all pretty much the same as standard recording.

One thing is *definitely* the same: the likelihood that you won't get it right on the first take. Sampling is tricky, especially when you're out to create an even, balanced multisound that blends smoothly over the entire keyboard. Be ready to try, and try again, as necessary.

It's as hard to make good sample as a good recording. The gravy comes when you succeed. That's when the real fun begins.

6

Sampling Rates and Resolutions

Waveforms, as we saw earlier, have two dimensions: time and acoustic energy. In sampling there are two dimensions as well—two different but equally important measurements called *sampling rate* and *sampling resolution*. Each plays a critical part in how good a digital recording sounds.

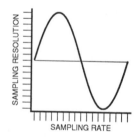

THE TWO DIMENSIONS OF SAMPLING

RATE is how many separate samples are measured each second.

RESOLUTION is how long a number is used for each measurement.

Film provides us with a useful analogy. If you consider each frame in a strip of film to be a single sample, then rate is how fast those frames were exposed, and resolution is their focus. Once more we find ourselves dealing in trade-offs. If a film's focus is perfect but its rate is slow, we see individual frames going by, one by one, and the illusion of reality is shattered. Conversely, if the rate is fantastic but the resolution is lousy, then we see a perfect reproduction of the world as it looks to someone in need of severe corrective lenses. Neither is what we want.

Proper reproduction of sound clearly requires the fastest sampling rate and the highest resolution we can muster...

...or does it?

We aren't done with trade-offs just yet. Remember memory? (Or, more properly, the lack of it?) If memory were infinite we'd have no problems. But it isn't. And the faster the rate and greater the resolution, the quicker memory gets eaten up.

A little math is necessary to make the point clear, but it's simple math, so don't worry.

Say you had 1000 index cards for memory storage, and you were allowed to put only a single digit (either 0 or 1) on each card. If each sample you recorded had a resolution of five cards, you'd run out of memory in 200 samples. Doubling the resolution to 10 cards immediately cuts the available samples in half, to 100. Of course, you could stretch those 100 samples to cover the same length of time as the earlier 200 did, by cutting the sampling rate in half as well; but the net result would be a gain of accuracy in one dimension at the expense of accuracy in another.

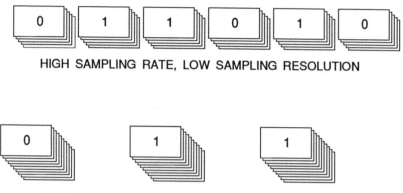

HIGH SAMPLING RATE, LOW SAMPLING RESOLUTION

HIGH SAMPLING RESOLUTION, LOW SAMPLING RATE

The trick is to find a combination of sampling rate and resolution that provides both good fidelity and useful recording time.

Here, thank goodness, the real world finally offers us some relief.

RATE RELIEF

All things considered, people don't hear very well. Most sounds contain overtone vibrations well up to 40 kHz (kHz is short for *kiloHertz*, an abbreviation meaning 1000 cycles per second), but even the very best human hearing doesn't go much above half of that: around 20 kHz. In fact, the upper hearing limit for and average adult is only 15 kHz, and if you live in a city count on it being even less.

There's plenty of sound up there, but we can't hear it. *And we never will.*

So why bother to reproduce it?

Enter Harry Nyquist, mathematician, with the answer. Nyquist proved conclusively that accurate reproduction of any sound, no matter how complicated, required a sampling rate no higher than twice as high as the highest frequency that could be heard. This means that high fidelity (as average ears define it) requires a sampling rate of only 30 kHz, and even the best ears need no more than 40 kHz. (CDs use a sampling rate of 44.1 kHz, which is one reason a well-engineered CD sounds awesome.)

As you use samplers you'll run into the term *Nyquist Limit*. That's the other side of the coin. As sampling rate lowers, so does the Nyquist limit—that is, the highest frequency that can be accurately reproduced. Sample something at a rate of 10 kHz and you won't get back anything higher in pitch than 5 kHz (with the possible exception of digital noise, which will be discussed in the next section). For low-frequency sounds, that might be good enough. But anything else would wind up sounding squashed; useful for special effects, maybe, but that's all.

RESOLUTION RELIEF

Here we are saved by fifth-grade math. You may or may not remember fiddling with *powers of two* in school, but they're certainly worth a look at now.

Computers such as the microprocessor inside your sampling instrument deal strictly in 0's and 1's, representing larger numbers through combinations of those two digits. Each digit is referred to as a *bit*; bits are combined into units called *words*; and the number of bits in a word determines the range of possible numbers that that word can represent.

The powers of two tell us that every bit we add to a word doubles the range of the word. A two-bit word can be used to represent four numbers; a three-bit word, eight; a four-bit word, sixteen; and so on.

Samplers typically use 8-bit, 12-bit, or 16-bit words. An 8-bit word can measure 256 separate levels of audio energy. A 12-bit word can measure 4096. A 16-bit word can measure 65536. This is considerably more resolution than provided by an 8-bit word, and results in sampled waveforms of great accuracy. But the trade-off here is price.

THE JOY OF VARIABLE SAMPLING RATES

Not all sounds are created equal. So why should they all be sampled at the same rate?

A bass drum doesn't have the high-frequency content of a trumpet. If your sampler offers you a choice of sampling rates, you can effectively juggle available memory by using low sampling rates on sounds that don't need high rates in order to be recorded well.

Find out the upper frequency limit of the instrument or sound sources you want to sample, and then choose a rate just over twice as great. Doing it that way conserves memory—and efficient use of memory is the best way to work with your sampler.

7

Digital Noise

Digital instruments such as samplers don't have as many noise problems as analog instruments do, but that doesn't mean they are noise-free. Noise is with us always. You can't escape it—that would take rewriting the laws of physics—but you can learn to minimize it if you understand the three principal causes.

NOISE SOURCE #1

Noisy sounds, of course. Always make sure your samples are recorded without noise in the first place. This means sampling with care, and paying attention to the cues your sampler is giving you. Some LCD readouts, for example, provide a useful visual indication of the level of the audio input.

NOISE SOURCE #2

After bad sampling, the next biggest source of noise is called *aliasing*. Aliasing is what happens when you sample a sound that has frequencies above the Nyquist Limit—that is, more than half the sampling rate. With some slight exaggeration for effect, here's what happens:

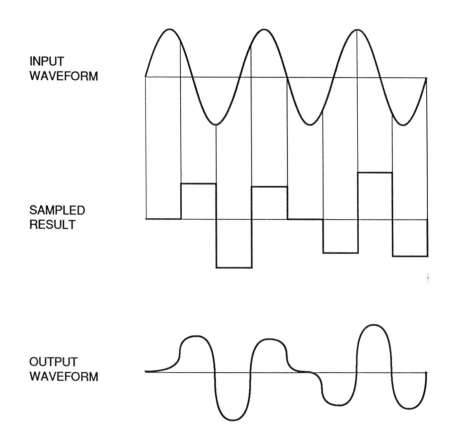

INPUT
WAVEFORM

SAMPLED
RESULT

OUTPUT
WAVEFORM

Above we see a sine wave being sampled slightly more than twice per cycle (i.e., the frequency of the wave is less than the Nyquist Limit), the digital waveform "picture" that results, and the reconverted waveform as it will sound when played. As you can see, the digital version isn't perfect, but it's close enough so that the DAC and the output filters can smooth it back into something reasonably close to the original.

But if we cut the sampling rate in half...well, take a look:

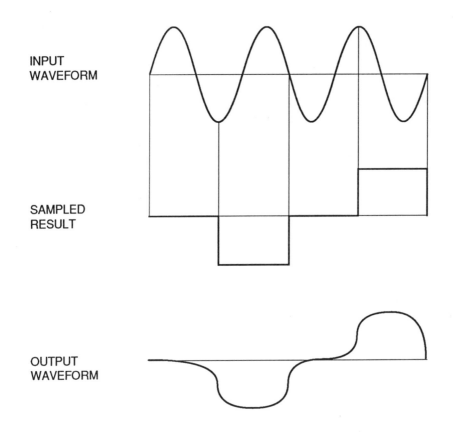

INPUT
WAVEFORM

SAMPLED
RESULT

OUTPUT
WAVEFORM

As you can see, the output waveform is now quite different from the source waveform. It has been *aliased*—given a new, lower pitch. This is bad enough with simple sine waves, but when aliasing happens to complicated waveforms the result is an unpredictable inharmonic noise that is generally unpleasant and unnatural in sound.

Samplers fight aliasing with input circuits called *anti-aliasing filters*. These are designed to block out any incoming frequencies that are above the Nyquist Limit, so that aliasing never happens. But the perfect filter has yet to be designed (that's a whole different set of compromises and trade-offs!), so you should still pay attention. Experiment with different sampling rates until you find the one that works best with a given type of sound. Or help out the input filters on your sampler by "prepping" a sound with the EQ on your mixing board, or with rackmount gear. (Another useful trick is to sample from a tape running at half speed, which is the equivalent of doubling your sampling rate).

A final note about aliasing noise: Sometimes you might actually want it! Just as analog distortion can enhance a guitar, certain sounds seem to improve with a hint of aliasing noise—sampled percussion, for instance.

NOISE SOURCE #3

The third source of noise comes from the "error component" created by the sampling resolution. Take a look at the following diagram:

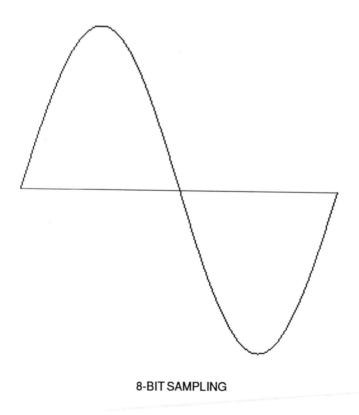

8-BIT SAMPLING

The digital representation of the original waveform isn't smooth, but stair-stepped. This is smoothed out when converted from digital data back into an audio signal, but not with absolute perfection, and the difference between input and output is noise. Generally speaking, the more bits used for sampling resolution, the less the noise.

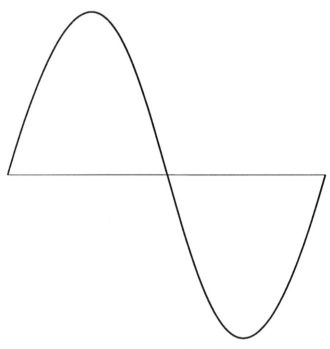

16-BIT SAMPLING

Compare the 16-bit digitized waveform with the 8-bit version. Clearly the 16-bit version is more accurate, and thus less noisy on output.

In traditional audio terms, you gain 6 dB of signal-to-noise ratio with every bit you add to the resolution. An 8-bit sampler like the original Emulator only had a 54 dB S/N ratio. A typical 16-bit sampler may have a S/N ratio in the area of 90 dB.

The best ways to compensate for noise from this source are the tried and traditional methods of proper signal level and proper EQ.

8

Pitch, Transposition, and Timbre

Sample a trumpet playing a C, and a C is what you've recorded. To make that note play back as a C# or an E or a C one octave up requires some pretty intense digital juggling. There are lots of different methods, and different samplers use different ones.

There's one thing they all have in common, though.

Right: trade-offs.

The basic fact is that our perception of timbre is tied very closely to pitch. A low piano A and a high piano A aren't separated just by frequency, but also by the radically different patterns of harmonics that are generated when the felt hammers of the piano strike strings of totally different groupings, types, and metals. It is not enough to sample one piano note and spread it over a whole keyboard. That won't work. The farther away from its original pitch any sampled sound is, the more distorted its timbre becomes. (The slang for this is *munchkinization*, the meaning of which should be obvious to anyone who remembers the munchkin singing in *The Wizard of Oz*.)

Furthermore, changing the pitch of a sample typically involves changing its length. If you drop two seconds of french horn down an octave by the simple trick of playing the samples back at half speed, they will take twice as long to go by. Playing them back at twice normal speed will raise the sound an octave, but it will also cut the total time in half. Sometimes tricks like this can make for useful effects (a growl sax sample transposed down four octaves sounds just like a small plane flying overhead) but they aren't often very musical.

For these obvious reasons, and several esoteric ones, creating what is *apparently* a single keyboard's worth of sound usually involves recording several *root samples,* each of which is assigned to a specific key. These root samples are then transposed up and down to fill out the keyboard, but only for a few notes in either direction, and their sounds are tailored so that they blend together well at boundaries.

How many root notes are needed to create an effective illusion depends in part on the relationship between pitch and timbral change in the instrument you are sampling, on how exacting you want to be, and how much memory you can spare for the task (remember, there's only so much available memory in your sampler, and it must be used with care).

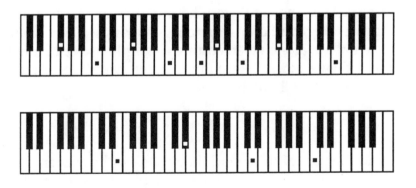

TWO DIFFERENT ROOT SAMPLE LAYOUTS

9

Truncating and Looping

One way to conserve memory is to not use any more of it than you have to.

Fortunately, some kinds of sounds—like drum hits—are short. Better still, it turns out that many sounds that aren't short have a lot of apparently critical information that *really isn't necessary at all,* so it can be disposed of and then faked.

Attacks are critical; they are overwhelmingly responsible for our perception of what kind of instrument is making a given sound, so best leave them alone when editing a sample (except for cutting off any silence at the beginning that you hadn't meant to capture). After that, all you have to do is:

1. Find the part of the sound that cycles without changing very much. Some samplers let you play back selected portions of a sample, to help isolate the part you want.

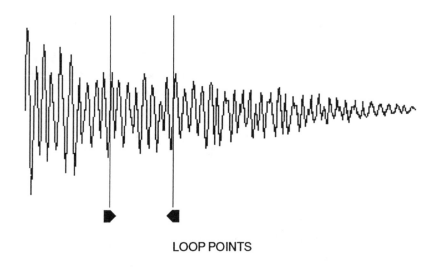

LOOP POINTS

2. *Truncate* (cut off) everything after it. (Depending on the sampler you own, don't do this lightly; with some, making a change like this is permanent. With others, you can change your mind about truncate and loop settings at any time.)

TRUNCATED WAVEFORM

3. Set the repeating portion to *loop* (repeat) for as long as you hold down the key. Net result? Even a half-second of string sample can be turned into massed strings that you can hold down for as long as you like.

Of course, there are all kinds of tricks to getting a loop right. With early samplers it was quite difficult to get glitch-free looping. More recent instruments make it a lot simpler, with built-in options for automatically searching out the best loop points, and *cross-fading* (blending) loops that still aren't quite right.

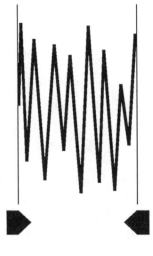

GLITCHED LOOP

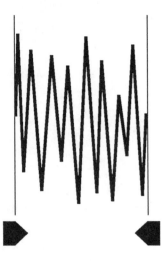

GLITCH-FREE LOOP

For even more powerful loop control and editing, you can buy a special kind of computer software called a *visual sample editor*. More on that in section 13.

10

Taking Samples Farther

An instrument that played samples back exactly as they were recorded, with no variation and no life, wouldn't be a very useful instrument! Because of this, most samplers offer features that let you put your samples through changes beyond the basics of truncating, looping, fading, and so forth. Some of these features—like programmable VCAs and VCFs—will be familiar to you because they have been standard on synthesizers for years. Others, only possible because of the digital nature of sampling, will be brand new. But all are useful, and if you want to get the most from your investment you should explore them.

The trick is to have two different kinds of memory: one for *sounds*, and one for *programs*.

To make the concept clearer, let's take a look at how a typical sampler generates and then modifies sound.

The sound memory in a sampler is a collection of *multisounds*. A multisound is made of one or more sampled sounds or synthesized waveforms (or even both at the same time) that have been truncated, looped, and tuned for best effect, then assigned to locations and ranges across the keyboard. What you do with the arrangement of a multisound is entirely up to you. You can select and blend together root samples from a single instrumental source, like a cello, so that the sampler becomes a cello across the length of its keyboard. You can take many different drum and percussion sounds and arrange them so that the sampler sounds like a complete kit. Some instruments even allow you to create your own waveforms, to sound just like a top-flight synthesizer (either digital or analog, depending on the waveform structures you choose). Or you can combine samples and waveforms, making the best of both approaches.

But these are just the beginning. What you color and shape your multisound with are the *synthesizer settings* stored in the separate *program* memory. With them, you can completely alter the shape, texture, and feel of what you hear.

Lengthen the attack of the VCA and you can make percussive sounds like pianos and drums bow as if they were cellos. Lengthen the release of the VCA and each note will linger like a fading choir (try that with timpani!) when you lift your fingers from the keys. Slow LFO modulation and a little oscillator detuning gives any sound a "rotating speaker" effect. Turn a glorious concert grand into a tinny honky-tonk upright by opening the VCF wide; make it into a proper accompaniment for "The Anvil Chorus" by closing the VCF down. Play the same sound over both DCOs, but detuned (either slightly, for rich digital flanging and chorusing, or to specific intervals, for harmony effects). EQ sounds to bring them out in a mix, or to give them new life and uses: an altered Japanese koto, for example, makes a surprisingly fresh-sounding funk bass. Give a sampled teakettle the characteristic pitch attack of a trumpet by programming in an automatic auto-bend. Add or reduce noise. Mix sounds together by subtly adjusting the ratio of their volumes. Make a harpsichord that is velocity-sensitive. Then turn up the VCF resonance and apply velocity sensitivity to the VCF envelope, so that it "wahs" when you want it to. Use built-in digital delay lines to bounce and echo sounds in all manner of ways, including feedback and crossfeed loop effects…

The possibilities really are virtually endless. What you can do with sampling is tremendous. But what you can do with sampling and creative *modification* of those samples is just plain staggering.

To benefit most from this separation of sound and program memory, you should make a point of keeping separate *library* and *performance* disks. Keep your samples, drawn waveforms, additive synth sounds, and useful programs on archived library disks. They are your raw material; the unmixed tone colors you'll use in painting your musical canvases. Program them as needed and store the results (for quick access) on performance disks. A single sound might very well be good for a hundred different variations, some subtle and some extreme. You'll never know until you try!

11

Juggling Memory

It's been said before in this book, but it should be said again:
Memory is the most important resource your sampler has. To get
the most out of your instrument, you must learn to use it well.

These are the four basic rules of memory juggling:

1. Never use a higher sampling rate than you have to.

2. Never use more root samples than you have to.

3. Never use longer samples than you have to.

4. GET RID OF WHAT YOU DON'T NEED. This is where
   keeping separate performance and library disks will be
   particularly useful. Your library disk samples should be
   sacred. Don't chop them up or throw them away, so you
   always have the sound there to play with if you need it.

But on performance disks, be ruthless. If you know you only need
the first two seconds of a five-second sound to get the effect you
want, throw out the last three. Otherwise they are taking up
memory space that would be better used for another sound.

12

Knowing What to Play

A sampler plays real sounds…but if your goal is to effectively imitate a wide variety of instruments, you have to keep *style* in mind, too.

Here are just a few examples:

- A clarinet can only play one note at a time. So when you play a sampled clarinet you should play single lines, not chords.

- The types of chords and runs played on a guitar are different than those typically played on a keyboard, because of the differing layouts of the two instruments. To fake guitar parts, you should force yourself to play the same notes a guitarist would, with the same little touches of personality: sharper attacks on certain notes, bent notes at specific points in a phrase, etc.

- Drummers typically keep steady patterns going with their feet and then play with (or against) those patterns with their hands. To do much the same, assign your bass and high hat samples to a part of the keyboard played by your left hand, and your tom, snare, and cymbal sounds to a part of the keyboard played by your right. Then maintain a steady pulse with your left hand, for time, and play alternating patterns with your right, for feel. The key is to think in blocks of patterns, like a drummer, instead of flowing chords and melodies.

Don't be afraid that imitating other instruments will stifle your creativity. Far from it! First, it will be a constant challenge to your technique, and challenge is how you grow. Second, you'll learn a lot about elements of music and arranging you probably have taken for granted up until now.

On the other hand, don't be content to *just* imitate other instruments. Samplers are a whole new technology, and that technology should be explored. Musicians with the imagination and daring to experiment will discover sounds and playing styles never before dreamed of...and have a lot of fun in the bargain.

13

Sample-Editing (and Creating!) Software

Probably the best way to supercharge your sampler is to hook it up to a computer. Why? Because adding a computer gives you a big monitor screen and a ton of extra processing power. Throw in good sample-editing software, and wonderful things become possible.

Here are just a few of the benefits to be gained:

- Complete visual display of your sounds, from overviews down to zoom-ins on waveform sections less than a thousandth of a second long.

- Easy cut-and-paste editing.

- Simple, glitch-free looping.

- Digital mixing for precisely blended effects and the creation of hybrid sounds.

- Digital equalization and signal-to-noise optimization, for improving the sound quality of samples.

- Complete remote control, with easy-to-read graphic displays, over the parameters of the sampler.

- FFT (Fast Fourier Transform) analysis and 3-D display of your sounds.

- Sound portability. You can take files originally from one brand of sampler and play them on another.

14

Glossary

ADC:

Analog-to-Digital Converter. The circuitry in the sampler that actually does the "sampling," i.e., that takes the original analog audio signal and changes it into the 0's and 1's of digital data.

ADDITIVE SYNTHESIS:

An approach to synthesis where complex waveforms are created by combining simple harmonics of differing volumes.

ALIASING:

A type of error that occurs during analog-to-digital conversion whenever there are frequencies greater than half the sampling rate. Such frequencies are misinterpreted, causing false information to be added to the data.

ALIASING NOISE: The false (and therefore inharmonic) frequency and waveform information generated by aliasing.

BIT: Short for **B**inary dig**IT**. A number that can have one of two values: 0 or 1. Samplers, computers, and other digital devices convey information using these bits, often combining them into *words*.

CYCLE: The repeating portion of a pitched audio waveform.

DAC: Digital-to-Analog Converter. The circuitry in the sampler that takes the sampled data and converts it from 0's and 1's back into an analog signal that can be amplified and heard.

GLITCH: A click, pop, or "jerk" in a sample, usually caused by inexact looping.

HARMONIC: A frequency component of a sound higher in pitch than the fundamental of that sound. The relative proportion of various harmonics is responsible for the timbre (tone color) of a sound.

INPUT FILTER: An anti-aliasing filter built into most samplers to cut out all frequencies higher than half the sampling rate. Any frequency higher than half the sampling rate will be misinterpreted when sampled, generating false harmonics known as aliasing noise.

KILOHERTZ (abbr. kHz): A measurement of frequency, indicating one thousand cycles per second.

NYQUIST LIMIT: The highest frequency that can be accurately reproduced by any given sampling rate (theoretically one-half the rate, though in practice a little less).

RAM: Random-Access Memory. RAM is empty until data is stored in it, and that data, once stored, can be edited and changed. It is also "volatile"; that is, it must be charged by a backup battery or else the data will be lost when the power to the instrument is shut off.

ROM: Read-Only Memory. The information in ROM chips is "burned in"; that is, it is stored permanently and can't be altered or erased.

SAMPLING RATE: The number of times per second the acoustic energy in a sampled sound is measured.

SAMPLING RESOLUTION: The number of data bits used to measure each individual sample.

WAVEFORM: A visual representation of the changing patterns of air pressure that make up a sound.

WORD: A string of *bits* used to convey a piece of information. In a sampler, each word comprises a single sample. Words are measured by the number of bits they contain (8-bit, 12-bit, 16-bit, etc.). In general, the longer the word, the higher the sampling resolution.